felt

felt

Sabine Fouchier

A & C Black ■ London

Dedication

To my parents, for their limitless love and support.

First published in Great Britain in 2008
A & C Black Publishers Limited
38 Soho Square
London W1D 3HB
www.acblack.com

ISBN-13: 978-0-7136-8494-0
Copyright © 2008 Sabine Fouchier

CIP Catalogue records for this book are available from the British Library and the U.S. Library of Congress.

Book design: Susan McIntyre
Cover design: Sutchinda Rangsi Thompson
All photographs & illustrations by Eric Doutreleau
© 2007
Commissioning Editor: Susan James
Copyeditor: Julian Beecroft
Proofreading and index: Sophie Page

Typeset in 10 on 13pt Myriad Light
Printed and bound in China

contents

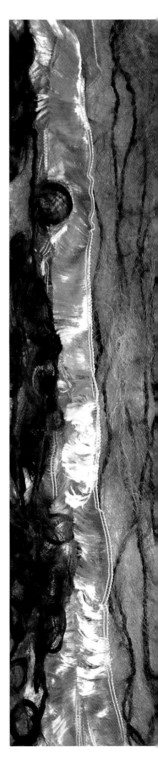

introduction

Natural materials have always fascinated me. My passion for beautiful textures and harmonies of colour goes back to my childhood. My mother was a good needlewoman, surrounded by elegant friends always eager to wear unique designs. I remember magnificent days spent discovering silk, *crêpe de Chine*, wool and other fascinating materials! Thus my designer's life was sketched out from a young age.

When it came to my education in Paris, in the milliner's studios of Marie Mercier, felt was imposed upon me from the very beginning. While moulding my first felt hat, with steam on a wooden hat block, I was possessed by a feeling of immense pleasure. At the end of my studies, I worked in Paris at La Boutique à Chapeaux, in the rue de Courcelles, where we made only unique, bespoke hats. It was a magic place for me! There, I had the pleasure of honing my professional skills with milliners who had practised for more than 40 years. The felt we used was bought from wholesalers and made in factories. The quality was great, but the choice of colours and patterns was very limited.

When I began to work independently, I decided to create designs for unique and very original hats. It was thus that I began making my own felt cones. I have now been a milliner and textile designer for more than ten years. I make hats, scarves, bags and shoes, all by hand with love and patience. Today I feel even more enjoyment in what I create.

Felt fascinates me! Being without weft, it is perfectly adapted to the work of a milliner, and for this reason has become essential in my work. It offers me unlimited possibilities, and as such it represents my ideal material. It is the very essence of textile!

My passion for this medium has brought me on numerous occasions to Mongolia, where I had the pleasure and the honour to interview Dr Batchuluun, historian and writer of Felt Art of the Mongols. He spoke at length to me about the origin of felt in Central Asia – the appendix at the end of this book is a brief overview of the place of felt in Mongolian culture, as related to me by Dr Batchuluun.

Felt is much more than just a fabric. It connects us with the earth, the animals, the sky and our sense of the sacred. I think of it as magical, captivating and friendly. It has always protected people from the cold, the rain, the wind, the arrows and the spirits. It tells the story of human beings, their evolution and way of life. Writing this book is my way of honouring this precious, noble and ancestral natural material. Through the following pages of history, personal techniques, ideas and inspirations, I hope to inspire and give the tools to any readers seeking to discover and perfect the art of felt.

If you are such a reader, be curious and daring. Felt is a forgiving material which allows the creation of new textures. On no account can you go wrong! It is also a material that allows you to express yourself freely in two or three dimensions, to be both painter and sculptor.

The book is a guide but you are the one who will make the discoveries. Very often we learn a lot from our mistakes. To move forward in felt-making, it is good to practice regularly.

Above all, felt-making is simple. The tools and materials are inexpensive and easy to acquire. The workshop can be the kitchen table, as long there's a sink nearby.

Felted wool is an incredibly flexible material – hard-wearing, insulating and capable of being shaped into any form. Felt is made not only from sheep's wool but also from the fleeces of other animals such as camels, yaks, goats or even rabbits. The felting rate of these fibres varies and can be far lower than wool. However, it is well worth testing them. For instance, yak wool is particularly soft and easy to felt. Moreover, plant fibres such as bamboo, cotton, soybean and flaxseed, as well as synthetic fibres, can be felted to varying degrees, though only when mixed with animal fibres. The products of these experiments are often very interesting and can lead to innovative and unusual textures.

acknowledgements

My special thanks to Dr Luntengiin Batchuluun, who shared with us his passion and knowledge, and to Nyamaa Shurkhuun, for her time and precious help in translating the interview. Also to my partner and my daughter for their great support, and to Rachel and Richard for their help and friendship. Finally, thanks to all the wonderful artists working in felt for supplying photographs and for sharing their artistic vision.

1 wool

To be interested in felt is to be interested in wool. Woollen fibre is the most common in the world, and of all the natural fibres it is also the best, with its unique characteristics and many uses. No synthetic fibre can replace it. Wool is a renewable raw material, 100% biodegradable and incredibly versatile. It needs very little energy to turn it into felt. In addition, felt-making, being such a simple, eco-friendly manual technique is an excellent form of therapy for people with autism or with motor problems caused by other conditions. It's also rare to have an allergy to wool, as the same protein, keratin, that is found in wool is also found in human hair, nails and skin.

There are between 600 and 2000 fibres per centimetre of wool, which accounts for its marvellous insulating qualities. One of its essential characteristics is what is known as 'curling', which is measured by the number of ripples per centimetre. For instance, 120 ripples per 10 cm (4 in.) denotes the finest fibre, whereas the largest would register only 12 ripples by 10 cm (4 in.).

The fineness of wool is measured in microns (μ), of which there are 1000 in every millimetre. Fibres measuring between 15 and 18 μ indicate a very fine wool; between 18 and 23 μ, a fine wool; and between 23 and 40 μ they indicate a coarse wool. In comparison human hair is about 75 to 80 μ. In the last ten years wool has become even finer. Nearly 40% of Australian production is below 19.5 μ. Indeed, fineness has become something of an obsession for many – there is now a World Wool Record Challenge, which rewards the farmer who produces the finest wool. In 2007 the record was 11.6 μ!

More than 1000 varieties of wool are available in different degrees of fineness and with different individual characteristics. There are different ways of classifying the types of wool obtainable from various sheep breeds. The British Wool Marketing Board divides the wool of just British sheep alone (of which there are more than 60 breeds) into seven different types: fine, medium, cross, hill, mountain, naturally coloured and lustre. All these types of wool have unique characteristics that dictate their ultimate use. The coarse wool of Hill and Mountain breeds such as Beulah or Blackface, for example, is used for making fine tweeds and carpets. Fine wool from Downland breeds such as the Oxford Down, for example, is used for hand-knitting and for making fine cloths, though even this fine British wool is not as fine as the merino wool used in the felting projects featured later in this book.

The development of wool

Wool comes from the fur or fleeces of various mammals, including sheep, goats, camels and even rabbits native to regions across the globe. Wherever human beings have kept animals they have used them as a source of energy, a means of transport and a source of both food and the raw material with which to make clothing and shelter.

The ovine tribe is made up of members of the genus ovis, comprising the mouflon (which first appeared about 2 million years ago in the region of modern-day Iraq) and its domesticated form, the sheep. There are five species of mouflon but only one species of domesticated sheep. However, this single species is distributed worldwide and represented by more than 200 breeds, between them adapted to various extreme environments. The quality, quantity and even the colour of wool produced depends on the breed and the health of the animal, but is also affected by the country, the region and especially the climate. Perhaps surprisingly, a cold climate with meagre pasture produces a better fleece.

The wool of merino sheep has an amazing quality, and accounts for 40% of the total global production of wool. Merino sheep are abundant in Australia, New Zealand and South Africa. The quality of a woollen fibre is defined by the fineness, length, strength, resilience, curl and uniformity of the fibres in a particular fleece. The fibre in merino wool is ultra-fine and has all the previously mentioned advantages of wool. It allows the production of a thin and lightweight fabric that is a veritable second skin with a high insulating power. Even after several washes it remains soft.

This type of wool is bound to a particular configuration of hair and fluff in the sheep. Unlike that of any other breed, merino hair fleece has the same quality and structure as the underfur. Its fleece is made up of more than one hundred million fibres. Each of these fibres grows at 2 mm per day and its diameter can vary from 10 to 70 μ. Each merino sheep produces the equivalent of some 9000 km (about 5600 miles) of fibre per year.

In modern wool production, however, even these natural advantages are not left to chance. In New Zealand, for instance, computers and hereditary factors are used to produce uniformly fine wool – a case of finding ideal partners for their sheep. The farmers even go as far as dressing the sheep to keep them clean, as this will yield some 3.5% extra wool. Naturally, for the sake of efficiency they have sought to automate as much of the sheep-shearing process as possible. They are even trying to soften the fleece to allow the wool to be withdrawn as easily as a Velcro strip. Moreover, the latest wools seek to amplify wool's natural isotherm quality. Plans also exist to introduce genetically engineered sheep, modified to produce the best wool. Clearly, the sheep is no longer dependent on just good pasture.

The qualities of fleece

A fleece is made up of all the hair from the same sheep, comprising two types: the thin, wavy short hairs that provide thermal insulation; and the jar, the surface hair, which is longer and coarse, and whose function is to protect from the wind and rain. It is held together by two substances, both of which give wool a more or less even coating: cholesterol or fat, produced by the sebaceous gland, known as suint; and grease, known as lanolin, which comprises steratine, oleine and especially potash (representing 30% of the total weight of the fleece).

Fleece does not have a uniform quality. The best wool, cut from live sheep, is found on the shoulders and sides; then the neck and thighs provide the next-best quality; and finally the tail and legs provide the poorest-quality wool, used in mattress padding.

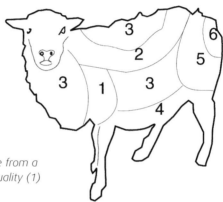

The qualities of wool obtainable from a fleece, ranging from the best quality (1) to the poorest (6).

An adult sheep produces between 2 and 8 kg of wool per year, two-thirds of which will comprise impurities – straw, mud, etc. A good fleece is tight, clean, thin, elastic, rich in grease and smooth to the touch. A bad fleece is open, dry, coarse and filthy, and the wool is brittle and hard.

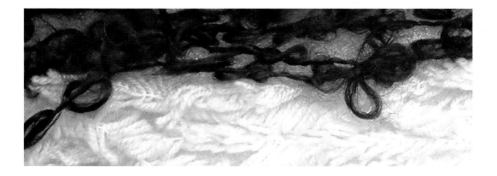

Wools and animal fibres of the world

Throughout history and in almost every continent, human beings have found ways of turning the hair or fleeces of their domesticated animals into fibres used in making clothing and other items. According to archaeological evidence, the sheep was first domesticated in Iraq in about 9000 BC. The various kinds of wool obtainable from sheep are:

- mouflon, a fibre from a wild sheep, similar to the one provided by the common sheep.
- merino, a high-quality fleece from merino sheep. The fibre has a very small diameter, and thus it is softer than most wool.
- lambswool, a fine and soft wool from the first shearing of a seven-month-old lamb.
- Shetland, a fibre which comes from the Shetland Islands, from a small sheep with a soft and silky fleece.

Goats were first domesticated in Persia in around 7000 BC, resulting in two types of hair still used for luxury textiles:

- angora, a longhaired, silky fibre obtained from goats from Asia Minor (a region close to Ankara, the capital of modern-day Turkey), from which mohair is obtained. This is not to be confused with angora wool from the angora rabbit.
- cashmere, a shorthaired fibre that produces wool of the utmost softness. It is obtained from goats living in the Kashmir Valley and Mongolia, and was first discovered by Europeans in the 17th century. The most precious cashmere is pashmina, also called 'golden fibre', and comes from the Himalayan mountain goat, or Chyangra, found in the Himalayan highlands. The delicate fibres are treated with rice starch to avoid them breaking. In theory goats are not sheared, but the explosion of global demand for cashmere and pashmina has led the Chinese in Inner Mongolia to raise herds of goats which are sheared. It takes up to ten goats to make a single stole, but the fibres do have a very high insulation quality. Pashmina and cashmere raw materials are scarce. The global production corresponds to 0.5% of that of sheep's wool. This breed of goats is not as expandable as most sheep, and can live only in very specific climatic conditions.

The Bactrian camel was first domesticated in the historical region of Turkestan in 3000 BC. The hair taken from camels living in the highlands of China and Mongolia produces a flexible fibre. Camel-hair fibres are used in overcoats and sportswear.

The yak, first domesticated in Tibet in about 2500 BC, is a ruminant with a long silky fleece. Yak hair can vary in colour from white through beige or grey to brown or black, the white hair being the most prized, as this can be dyed. The animal still lives among human communities in modern-day Tibet and Mongolia.

The llama, which was first tamed in the Andes in South America in around 5000 BC, produces a long beige-coloured fibre. The alpaca, like its close relation the llama, is a member of the camel family and was brought into domestic use around 1000 years later. Its name comes from a Peruvian word meaning 'animal of the Andes', where it was one of the treasures of the ancient Incan civilization. Alpaca hair can be any one of more than 20 different shades, including white, beige, brown, grey and black. It is a shiny, fine

and soft fibre. Alpacas are a cross between vicuñas and guanacos, which were domesticated some 7000 years ago. Today the fibre is used to make knitwear and accessories such as shawls and stoles.

The rabbit was first domesticated in France as recently as 600 BC. The Angora rabbit, originally from Turkey, gives up a soft and warm fibre that is very expensive, and as such is often mixed with other fibres.

Wool fibres are also obtained from:

- the guanaco, a small wild Andean llama, which has been bred successfully in Europe. It's the only animal with a fleece made up entirely of fine-quality fibre, similar to cashmere.
- the cashgora, a goat found in New Zealand, a crossbreed between the angora and cashmere goats. Cashgora combines the smoothness and softness of cashmere and the shine of mohair.
- the vicuña, a member of the llama family and the smallest of the camelids, most commonly found in the higher parts of the Andes in South America (Ecuador, Bolivia, Peru and northern Argentina). Vicuña fibre is regarded as the finest animal fibre in the world, comparable to silk. During the Inca period the fibre was reserved exclusively for royal use. It has not been possible to domesticate this animal, which nowadays is protected by conservation measures.

The most sought-after wools are merino, mohair, cashmere and alpaca.

Turning fleece into wool

SHEARING

This usually happens once a year, in spring, but it can also be done a second time, in September. The fleece is cut using special scissors by hand or by electrical shears. The fleece is cut in a specific sequence so as to hold together in one piece. A professional can shear a sheep in less than three minutes

SORTING

Fleece fibres are classified according to the quality of the wool and the various parts of the sheep. Fibres are sorted by length, fineness, elasticity, colour, uniformity, cleanliness and strength.

WASHING

The grease or lanolin in the wool causes dust and the remains of leaves to adhere to the fleece. These, along with the suint, need to be removed before the wool can be used. Before washing it is necessary to open the fleece, airing it so that any impurities such as mud and straw can fall out. This is done using a wool-scouring machine.

Washing reduces the weight of the fleece by about 40%, and partially removes the lanolin, the substance that renders the wool extremely smooth and waterproof for the sheep. First the fleece must be soaked in water, to remove any remaining impurities.

Then the grease is scraped off and collected up. The fleece is rinsed with water, and then all the water is squeezed out and the fleece left to dry. After washing, between 0.5 and 0.8% of the lanolin should remain in the fibres, to give them flexibility. In modern sheep-farming the fleece is sometimes also plunged into a bath of sulphuric acid to reduce the extraneous dust and plant material, and thence into a neutralisation bath.

The grease is recovered and refined to be put to various industrial uses in pharmaceuticals (ointment), steel (lubricant) and beauty products, under the name of lanolin.

CARDING

To disentangle the fibres, they need to be brushed (carded) in the same direction in order to separate them. To do this, either carding machines fitted with rollers, or hand brushes with metal spikes can be used. The process of carding also eliminates any impurities.

The cleaned wool can then be felted or spun.

felt

Felt is the oldest-known textile. It existed long before the inventions of weaving and knitting. It is a non-woven fabric made from animal fibres, mainly sheep's wool, the arrangement of whose fibres is not organised.

Each woollen fibre has small scales on its surface, in the same way as human hair. The scales all overlap each other, like roof tiles. The felt-making process is simple. When you pour hot water onto wool, the scales open up. Then by rubbing or rolling the wool the scales interlock and close up, creating a strong fabric which doesn't fray when cut.

There are two types of felt, whose methods of manufacture in both cases use the scales on the fibres to entangle and hold them together.

(NB: An intentional narrowing of a knitted fabric is called felted or boiled wool – this can be done industrially or by hand).

Under a microscope the disorganised intermingling of fibres in wool felt can be clearly seen.

HANDMADE FELT

The wet technique uses hot water, soap and friction to entangle and amalgamate the fibres. The dry technique uses a needle with sharp barbs to poke the fibres, in order to create a fabric or a sculpture.

INDUSTRIAL FELT

Synthetic fibres appeared for the first time in the 19th century, under the name of rayon. Today the science of petrochemistry has provided us with thousands of different types of fibres. Felt produced by industrial process can be made from natural or synthetic fibres. The chemicals allow all types of fibres to be made into felt, even those without any scales. For instance, the felt used for craft making is often comprised of wool mixed with acrylic or polyester.

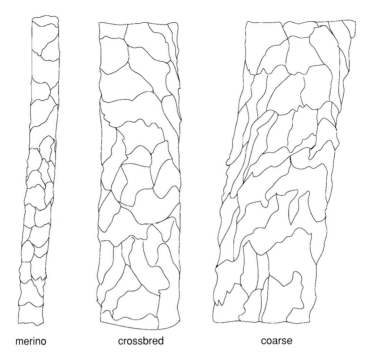

| merino | crossbred | coarse |

The various types of wool fibre differ greatly in thickness and quality, as this drawing made from a microscopic image makes clear.

The main method of producing non-woven fabrics is to use a needle machine, originally designed for the manufacture of bedcovers. This machine uses small, hooked needles which mix and stick the fibres by repetitively poking the surface.

Its characteristics

ABSORPTION

Wool is porous and permeable, and one of the most hydrophilic fibres. It can absorb up to 33% of its weight without being wet to the touch and while retaining its insulating effect. By comparison the absorption rate of cotton is 8% and that of synthetics less than 5%. As moisture is absorbed by fibres heat is produced, and vice versa – moisture loss is accompanied by heat absorption.

ELASTICITY

If stretched, wool fibres will return to their original form when released. This is the memory of fibre. Each fibre has a constant elasticity and the ability to resume its shape, referred to as resilience. Wool can be subjected to over 20,000 torsions without breaking, whereas silk breaks at 8000 and rayon at 75 twists. For this reason, felt is particularly useful in the manufacture of parts subjected to repeated use.

PERMEABILITY

Felt may be either permeable or impermeable to liquids and gases, depending on its density. Wool is used in the filtration of dust and gas, and the separation of solids and liquids.

RESISTANCE

Felt has a great resistance under pressure, and ages well. It is resistant to ultraviolet light, to steel, oils, solvents and even the most powerful acid, such as sulphuric acid. But beware – bleach is not to be used with felt, as it damages the fibres and can even dissolve them.

Wool only ignites at temperatures above 560ºC (1040ºF), and thus can be regarded as a fire retardant. It is also resistant to abrasion and repeated blows (e.g.: glossing stones and glass).

INSULATION

Wool is a high-quality insulator, offering natural protection from hot and cold conditions. As up to 80% of its total weight can be air, it is a powerful isothermal, naturally maintaining either warmth or coolness.

Felt is a very poor conductor of heat and electricity. Its outstanding qualities are maintained even when the temperature changes dramatically. It is also an excellent sound insulator.

PLIANCY

Felt can be moulded and stretched in any direction. When cut it does not fray.

Its uses

Felted wool is a high-quality product, on account of its basic characteristics, its feel to the touch and its adaptability. Easy to cut, it can be both sewn and glued; it can be shaped into numerous forms; it can be coloured and treated against fire and moths. It is also light- and soundproof.

There are different depths of felt: between 0.8 and 1.5 mm is referred to as very thin; and between 1.5 and 50 mm encompasses thin to thick.

Felt is used primarily in the clothing sector, where its applications are numerous: under collars, in coat linings, in dresses, purses, suits, slippers, shoes, hats and other items of clothing. The fibre is covered with silicon to enable it to be washed in the washing machine (see the Woolmark label) and to render it softer for dry-cleaning purposes.

Felt is also made into carpets, cushions, tents, boots, shepherds' cloaks and figurines. Made of felt and wood, the *yurt* or *ger*, the traditional round tent dwelling of Central

Asia, remains widespread. It is found in insulation, for instance in cars, railway carriages, and in house construction; in soundproofing (on the feet of a chair); in the protection of fragile materials such as glass during transportation; in sound absorption (the hammers in a piano); in the polishing of glass, marble and metal; and in the filters and joints used in domestic appliances.

In a scientific book dating from the Middle Ages, felt is said to resist iron and fire if first treated with vinegar!

Its history

Wool is a biodegradable material, and thus there are few traces left from ancient times. Nevertheless, the making of cloth is one of the earliest signs of human culture. The first evidence of felt is found in clothing from the Bronze Age. The felted wool from this period was a vast improvement on the skins that preceded it. From the time humans first realised how to remove animal hair using a knife, they began to interweave fibres to form a fabric, first with their fingers, then before long with the help of a loom.

Felt is the oldest way of working with wool. It has been known for about 3000 years. In 1947 eight funeral chambers were discovered in the high Altai mountains, between the Soviet Union, China and Mongolia, dating back to a period between the 5th and 3rd centuries BC. Scythian textiles were found (the Scythians were a nomadic people who lived between the 7th and 3rd centuries BC), and also tapestries, very well preserved by the ice, including the famous Tapestry of Pazyryk (today at the Hermitage Museum in St Petersburg, Russia). A wall-hanging found there was made of felt appliqué and decorated with human and animal figures. Many felt accessories, saddle pads, blankets, socks, bags, hair accessories for women, decorations and figurines were also discovered. Among the most interesting objects unearthed were some felt totemic idols. These are felted sculptures of swans and geese, filled with goat's hair and compacted until they were as hard as wood. Overall, these graves gave up the richest trove of textiles yet discovered, revealing the art and illuminating the everyday lives of these nomadic people, who for centuries had been preeminent across half the Asian continent. Moreover, felt is still an integral part of the lives of people in this region of the world. It is used in everyday life, as well as for ceremonies and rituals, and the decorative patterns favoured relate to the history of their ancestors, which for many centuries has been recorded in wool.

Felt seems to have reached Europe a few centuries later. There is known to have been a wool industry in Greece in 75 BC. The Greeks and the Romans, like the Chinese, used felt as padding under heavy armour, as lining for their helmets, and as protection against arrows (a thick felt garment stops an arrow better than leather). During the Roman occupation of the British Isles, in 50 AD a large wool-processing factory was established in Winchester, England. However, with the decline of the Roman Empire in Europe felt begin to disappear, and it was not until the Crusaders, who brought back the fabric from Constantinople, that it began to re-emerge. Gradually, during the 12th and 13th centuries, felt replaced leather and fur, which were costly to procure and did not always provide effective protection against rain, snow and wind.

The golden age of the use of felt in Europe was in the 15th century. The product was highly strategic in the foundation of a large textile industry, which was controlled by political power in England, France and Spain.

The exact circumstances of the discovery of felt remain a mystery, but many legends exist in the world and all seem to agree upon its accidental nature. In Europe St Clement, then a wandering monk, discovered that he could protect his feet by putting woollen fibres in his shoes. He noticed that the combination of his sweat and the friction that occurred while walking turned the wool into a firm sole. He later became bishop and improved the manufacturing technique, and today he is the patron saint of milliners.

The Persians tell the story of a man who was sure he could make a fabric without a loom. After several days of trying without having achieved his goal, he became angry and stamped on the wool, his tears dampening it as he ranted and raved. Thus felt was born!

Felt around the world

IRAN

Felt manufacture has lasted since ancient times because the Turkmen nomads in this region have continued to find a wide variety of everyday uses for it. Carpets, hats, shepherd's coats, water-pipe bags and under-saddles for horses, camels and donkeys are all traditional felt items. The main areas where the felt tradition continues are located in the north and the south of the country, among families who have always felted for themselves and their neighbours using their own wool. Sadly, however, the quality of these items has increasingly declined since the introduction of industrially produced felt.

AFGHANISTAN

In the 20th century, the thousands of nomadic Kuchi Uzbeks who came to Afghanistan from the former Soviet Union brought with them their felt tradition, which is notable in particular for embroidered felt. Many items are still made, even though the tribes have now adopted settled ways of life. In the north and west felt is still used to make yurts (large round tents), socks with rubber soles, rugs, blankets, bags, shepherds' cloaks and under-saddles.

TURKEY

Traditionally, felt in Turkey has meant the manufacture of carpets, hats (the *kulahs* worn by the Whirling Dervishes of the Sufi sect of Islam), bags, headdresses for camels and charms. But today the industry and the methods used for hundreds of years are disappearing; many felt guilds once existed in Turkey, but today there are only a small number. Indeed, the only felt item that is still widely made is the traditional hooded shepherd's cloak, called the *kepenek*. Made from wool or a combination of wool and goat hair, it is a very effective protection against strong winds and freezing temperatures.

IRAQ

Felt items are found in the mountainous north of the country, mainly in long and narrow mats made by women and in shepherds' coats that could have come from Turkey.

KAZAKHSTAN, UZBEKISTAN, KYRGYZSTAN, MONGOLIA, GEORGIA

It is mainly in these countries of Central Asia that the tradition of felt-making has survived until the present day. Yurts, rugs, decorative blankets for camels, boots, long capes (*burqas*), embroidered quilts, wall hangings and decorative objects are made from the fabric.

Felted with the help of a horse or a camel, it is ideal for the nomadic life and survival in freezing temperatures. There is also a strong tradition of sewn and embroidered felts of the same type as those found in the collection of Pazyryk. The Silk Road, which for centuries has stretched from Turkey to Mongolia, is dotted with yurts.

HUNGARY

A long felt-making tradition, from Central Asia is still to be found in Hungary.

Shepherds still today take shelter, as did their ancestors, under a *szür*, a calf-length felt coat. These cloaks can be worn as a coat during the day and a sleeping bag at night.

AFRICA

In Africa, felt is only to be found in the mountains of Morocco, in a tradition that probably emanates from Turkey. The traditional red felt hat, the *fez*, originated in the eastern Mediterranean during the Ottoman Empire. It is here in this climate that wool's more surprising quality is exploited, with Bedouin tribespeople wearing woollen clothes to combat the heat. By absorbing the sweat and slowly releasing it through evaporation, wool provides a pleasant coolness in summer as well as protection from the cold in winter. The Berber people, who can be found across this region of North Africa, also use felt wall-hangings for their ceremonies.

SCANDINAVIA

The felt tradition in Scandinavia is old, with felt fragments dating from the 5th century AD having been found. Scandinavian sheep, which can still be seen today with their distinctive short tails and multi-coloured fleeces, were also present at an early stage.

In Norway people produced felt waterproof boots (similar to Russian boots), shoe soles and hats. Working methods have not changed much since the first boots were made. In Sweden there are boots, shoes, gloves and hats made of felt, as introduced by the Lapp people in 1900. Felt was a tradition from the north, but it didn't spread further afield. In Lapland lots of clothes were made of felt, though today handmade felt has been replaced by felted fabric. In Finland felt made by hand was replaced as long ago as 1887 by a factory. The boots and socks made there were used by the Finnish Army and exported to Sweden and Canada.

Mongolian yurts.

 # basics

Materials and equipment

To make felt you will need:

- Wool: Merino tops (see glossary) and fancy yarns
- Soap: Any soap except pH neutral will do, but I would recommend olive oil soap, as it has a high pH difference from wool (more alkaline) and is kind to your hands.
- Plastic bowl
- Recycled plastic milk bottle
- Foam underlay (found in any DIY shop and used as underlay for laminate flooring)
- Bubble wrap (2 x 1 m/6 x 3 ft)
- Straw mat or towel for rolling
- Net curtain (1 x 1 m/3 x 3 ft)
- Comb for carding
- Felting needles in various sizes
- Scissors
- Sewing needles
- Threads
- Iron
- Sponge
- Hat block in wood or polystyrene (or a plastic bowl turned upside down)

You can also add to the wool natural fibres such as flax, soya, mulberry silk or gummed silk. Remember also that wool can be recycled – keep your leftovers as these can be felted again and again.

How to dye wool

The natural colours of wool include white, cream, light grey and dark brown, depending on the breed of sheep. For centuries natural dyes for wool have been procured from mineral oxides found in rocks, from fluids extracted from insects or shellfish, and especially from the maceration (the breaking down of fibres through soaking in liquid) of various plants. With plant dyes you should use mordants (metal oxide).

Synthetic dyes invented by chemists in the 19th century are today increasingly replacing colours that can be naturally obtained. They are easy to use, as the colour is ready and just needs to be mixed with water and brought to the boil. Some salt must be added to fix the colour, and the material should always be wetted before dyeing (always refer to the manufacturer's instructions on how to use them).

European knowledge of different natural dyes came from the Phoenicians in the Middle East in the 5th century AD. Their brightly coloured traditional costumes had symbolic meanings as well as being signs of affluence. Nowadays the traditional fabrics of South America, India and Africa are still coloured with natural dyes. For instance, in Mexico, a bright red is obtained from cochineal collected from aphids found on cactuses. Reds are also made using certain kinds of sandalwood chips. A very dense blue is made with indigo, which is grown in Egypt and Asia, while yellow is produced from onion peel and certain lichens. For the full range of browns, the bark and leaves of oak trees are used.

Soaking textiles in a bathtub of water in which dye has been dissolved is a traditional procedure, used in both industry and handicrafts. High-temperature dye baths give the best impregnation of the fibres; cold dyes are often less efficient. To obtain a quality dye, colouring must be distributed evenly through yarns and fibres. For colours to become attached to the fibres, they must undergo an attraction referred to as 'affinity'. This affinity is enhanced by the addition of chemicals such as alkaline salts, reducers (hydrosulphite soda) or carbon sulphides. Affinity also requires the use of certain colours with certain fibres, which may not work with others. Finally, mordants (metal oxides) are used with the plant dyes to fix the dye in the material.

From the red soil found in the graves, it is known that red ochre was used as a dye during the Paleolithic period. During the Neolithic period however, dyes were mainly extracted from plants.

Some examples of natural sources of dyes include: plant – roots, lichens, fruits, and indigo; animal – cochineal, various insects; mineral – cinnabar (vermilion). However, beware of false friends. Red fruits such as cherries, strawberries and raspberries do not dye. The same is true of blueberries, dandelion roots, beets and red cabbage.

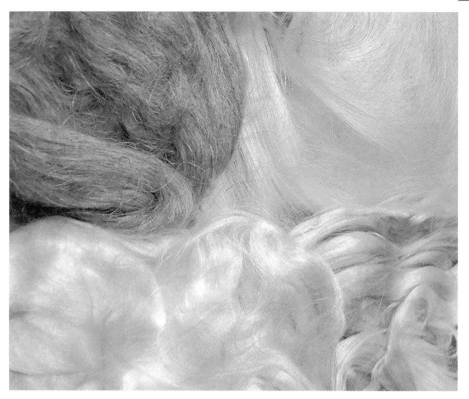

Gummed silk (top right), soybean (bottom right), flax (top left), mulberry silk (bottom left).

Wool can be dyed in fleece or in yarn.

The materials you will need for dyeing are:

- Gas stove
- Pot (enamel, aluminum or stainless steel)
- Glass jars (jam jars or other kinds)
- Wooden sticks (anything more or less the length of a chopstick)
- Kitchen scales
- Thermometer
- Spoons (both teaspoons and larger spoons)
- Rubber gloves

MORDANTS

Always first moisten the wool before dyeing. Mordants help the wool to retain the dye. They can be used either before or after dyeing, depending on the dyeing agent you're using. Alum, tin crystals, potassium dichromate, ferrous sulphate or copper are all viable mordants.

Mordant recipe with alum and cream of tartare (for use before dyeing)

In 1 litre (a little over 2 pints) of water, dissolve 9 g of alum and 3 g of cream of tartare needed. Boil this mixture for three minutes, then cool by adding 2 further litres (4¼ pints) of cold water. Then plunge the wet wool into the mixture. Bring it to a gentle boil and heat for one hour.

NB: If you need to set the wool aside for one or two nights, remove the mordant, dry and keep the wool away from the air.

DYE RECIPES

Beige
500 g oak acorns
200 g wool
Mordant for wool (see recipe)

Prepare the wool in the mordant bath. Cook the acorns in 1 litre of water for two hours to create a dye bath. Then remove the acorns and put the wool pieces in the dye bath. Finally, boil gently for one hour.

Yellow–orange
50 g onion peel
100 g wool
15 g alum

Method: In this recipe no mordant is used. Put the wool with the onion peel and the alum into 2.5 litres of hot water (it must be hot), and boil for one hour.

Basic techniques

Before you start the workshops, you need to practise making a simple flat piece of felt.

To begin with, the way you hold the fibres in your hand is essential. Hold the merino top in one hand and try to pull a length of wool, then try to pull a longer one. You must have the same amount of wool each time you pull the fibres. Start laying out your wool so that the new length overlaps the ends of the previous one by about a third, like roof tiles. Make sure that the wool fibres do not twist.

The picture describes the ideal position for the hands. Hold the wool in one hand at least 10 cm (4 in.) from one end. If you hold it too close to the end it will be very difficult to pull. With your other hand gently pull the fibres using the tips of the fingers and the base of the thumb. Repeat the gesture, keep your hands steady.

Obviously, it's crucial that you shouldn't be tense when making felt – quite the contrary. Relax!

When you pour hot water onto wool fibre, the scales open up. A felting agent, commonly either vinegar or soap, is used to disturb the pH of the wool, thus helping to bring up the scales. Then when you rub and roll it the scales interlock and close up, creating a strong fabric which doesn't fray when cut.

When pulling out the fibres you will see that at one end the fibres are thinner. By superimposing layers of fibres, each layer running in the opposite direction to the one below, you will ensure that your fabric does not have any holes or weak points.

How you apply pressure and how many times you roll the wool will affect how the felt turns out. In this regard, everyone has their own techniques – some use bubble wrap, some use a straw mat, others a towel or a combination of two or more. Feel free to use whatever works for you. It is important to use soap from the beginning of the process, and you should also bear in mind the temperature of the water, remembering that hot water tangles the wool more easily. For the final rinse, when the felt is done, the water must be cold as it helps the fibres to contract one more time.

Felt-making is a physical activity that requires a good position of the body, just as if you were playing sport. By the same measure, you also need to breathe.

Felt-making is also often compared to painting and drawing, as it offers a real freedom to design shapes and colours. It also offers definite advantages over painting: it dries very quickly – unlike oil paint, for instance – and colours can be mixed or removed very easily. Many artists love the freedom that this medium affords them to express their artistic vision. I myself find it very meditative.

In the first workshop you should aim to become familiar with the infinite potential of the wool by making a flat two-dimensional piece of felt in which you can express your imagination, just as if you were painting.

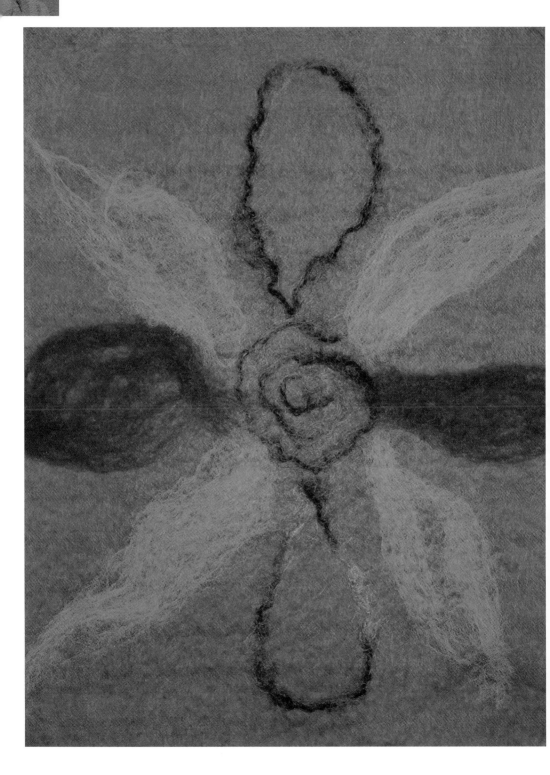

2-D: How to felt a flat piece

Before starting, cover your table with a plastic tablecloth, if necessary. Lay out your straw mat, then lay out the bubble wrap flat on top of it. The bubble wrap needs to be at least twice the size of the piece of felt you are trying to make, as it will later be folded over. The fibres are laid directly onto the bubble wrap.

1

1 Pull and spread the wool evenly in the same direction. Make your first layer by overlapping the layers of fibres in the manner of roof tiles in order to avoid any weakness in the felt. Form a square of about 30 x 30 cm (12 x 12 in.). When this is done, you should no longer be able to see the bubble wrap.

2

2 Spread another layer of wool across the first layer at 90º to the first. It helps if the tension is identical in both directions, so that the felt shrinks evenly.

3 Form the third and final layer by laying out the wool in the same direction as the first, i.e. at 90º to the second.

It is essential that these layers are as even and as thin as possible, to ensure a good-quality felt. So before going any further you need to check that no part is either too thick or too thin. If you find any that is, with your hands resting on the wool, feel if the fibres are arranged evenly, and either add or remove fibres until any weakness or unevenness has been eliminated.

3

4 Using coloured wool and yarn, begin to decorate the background. Take your time to play with design, using different thicknesses of wool and yarn.

4

5 The wool and yarn for the decoration can be positioned in any direction. I choose mohair yarn because it's very easy to felt with and has a diffuse effect that I really like. When you are happy with it, cover the wool with the synthetic net curtain. This will help to keep the design in place when you start to rub.

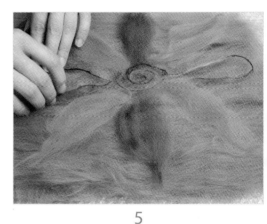

5

6 Take the plastic bottle and puncture the cap with several holes. Fill the bottle with hot soapy water and shower this on all the fibres. It should be evenly damp but not soaking wet.

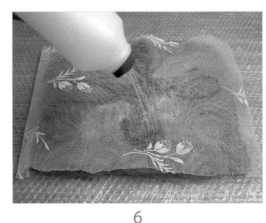

6

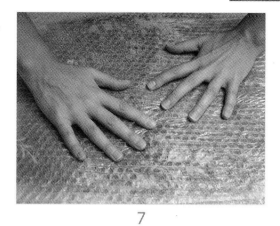

7 Press the wool gently with your hands, through the folded-over piece of bubble wrap. The fibres should feel flat and matted. When pressed, there should not be any air bubbles.

7

8 Next fold back the piece of bubble wrap. Put a lot of soap on your hands and slowly, with slight pressure, begin to rub the wool through the curtain.

8

9 Some fibres can get through the net. Lift the net to check whether this has happened, and pull gently, holding the wool with one hand. Then put the net curtain back in position and keep rubbing and massaging for ten minutes. When the decoration has adhered to the background, you can remove the net and cover the wool with the bubble wrap. Flatten it out.

9

10 Wrap the wool tightly in the bubble wrap and the straw mat. Roll it back and forth for several minutes, under slight pressure. Then unroll it, and flatten the fibres through the bubble wrap.

10

11 You need to keep changing direction as you roll the felt, so as to obtain a steady shrinkage. Turn the piece through 90°, wrap it up and continue to roll. Continue rolling until the felt is firm and difficult to stretch. Pinch it with your fingers to see if the fibres are properly felted. Pour on a little bit of hot water to moisten it and roll for a few more minutes.

11

12 The felt is now ready. Rinse with cold water until the soap has completely disappeared. You can add a drop of vinegar in the final rinse bath, as protection against moths. Then stretch your felt to its final shape and let it dry flat in a warm place.

NB: To obtain a smooth surface, iron the back of your piece of felt on the wool setting.

12

4 how to make a cushion

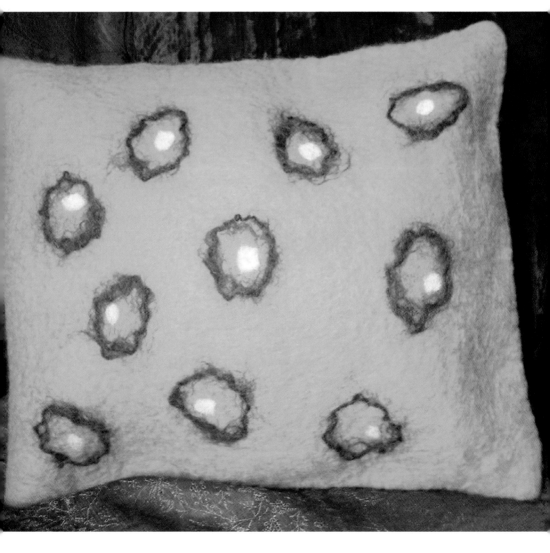

I love cushions! Easy to make, they embellish a room or a sofa. In this project we will make a 3D, one-piece seamless cushion, using pre-felted cuts to obtain strong patterns. One can imagine making all sorts of shapes and sizes using this technique. It can even be applied for a stylish evening clutch bag!

Use a similar template to that shown in this workshop or draw your own shape. Remember that wool shrinks, so always add 30% to the final size, in order to achieve the desired size pattern. Choose the colours of fleece you want (between 70 and 100g, but no more), prepare bits of pre-felt, and have some fancy yarns ready.

1 Design the size and shape of your cushion, bearing in mind that felt will shrink. Make one side of the shape longer to accommodate a flap. Cut out the template in foam underlay.

2 Spread your first layer of wool in a single direction over your template. Cover it completely overlapping the edges by 3 cm (1¼ in.), so as to be able to fold the 'seams'.

3 Lay the second layer over the first at 90°. Then spread the third layer in the same direction as the first.

4 Decorate your cushion by creating patterns with fancy yarns, natural fibres such as mohair and pre-felted pieces.

5 Place the net over the top and wet it with hot soapy water. It should be evenly damp but not soaking wet. If you put on too much water, mop it with a cloth or a towel. Cover with bubble wrap and, using both hands, press gently to flatten the fibres. There should not be any air bubbles.

6 Remove the net. Turn over your fleece and template in the bubble wrap, then carefully start to fold the fleece around the edges. Do not fold around the flap, as this will be cut at the end when dry, giving the cushion its final shape.

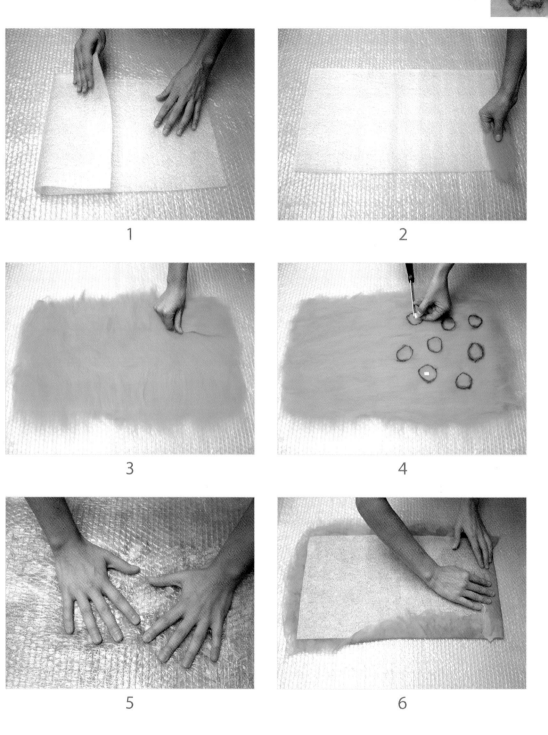

1

2

3

4

5

6

7 On this side, spread more wool over roughly two thirds of the template. Leave the opening and the flap free of wool. Lay three layers of wool across the template, changing directions between each one as before. This time there is no need to fold around the edges.

NB: A few fibres may overrun the edge of the template, but don't worry as we'll simply fold them over when we turn back to the front side.

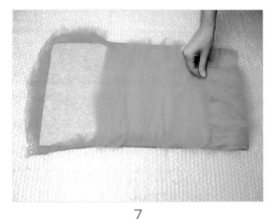

7

8 Now decorate the other side of the cushion as you wish. Place the net over the wool and start to wet it with warm soapy water.

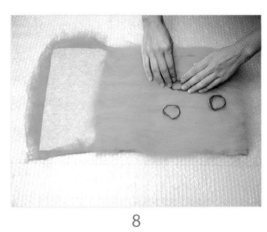

8

9 With soapy hands, rub the wool through the net gently for five minutes. Turn the wool over in the bubble wrap, holding it firmly and folding the edges if necessary. Cover it with the net and continue to rub gently for ten minutes. Lift up the net occasionally to prevent the fibres poking through.

9

10 Continue alternately rubbing both sides through the net for 15 minutes. Cover with bubble wrap and lightly massage the edges of the 'seams', carefully following the shape of the template.

10

11 Roll the fleece up tightly inside the bubble wrap and the straw mat. To obtain more pressure, tie the roll tightly with strips of fabric or elastic bands, usually one at each end and one in the middle. Then roll it back and forth 100 times. Then unroll and flatten it out, and wet it with more hot water. Turn the cushion through 90º and roll 100 times once more.

11

12 When the felt is starting to shrink, remove the template, then rub and flatten the edges using both hands. Use a lot of soap – this speeds up the rate of felting. Repeat the rolling process for a further ten minutes. If it is more comfortable, you can dispense with the straw mat and use just the bubble wrap for this part of the process.

12

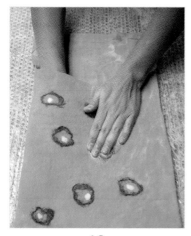

13

13 When the felt has shrunk by about 30%, stretch it into shape.

14

14 Rinse with hot water and roll it again, changing directions, until it feels firm and difficult to pull.

15

15 Your cushion is now fully felted! Rinse with cold water, eliminating all the soap. You can add a drop of vinegar to protect against moths. Throw your felted cushion ten times against the table.

16

16 Make a felted bead for the button using similar colours. You can cut it in two, if
desired. Create your buttonhole by cutting a short slit directly into the flap. Sew the
bead at the back. Draw the shape of the flap you want and cut.

how to make a bag

Bags: how many bags can a woman have? Never enough! This project is aimed at all those who dream of making a custom-made bag. You can imagine and make all kinds of shapes and sizes: with or without a flap? A stylish shopper or an evening bag? Some handles – long or short, one or two?

Here I chose to make a reversible bag using 140 g (5 oz) of wool, though thicker bags will need more. It can be slung over the shoulder as well as carried in the hand. I also added a very handy pocket.

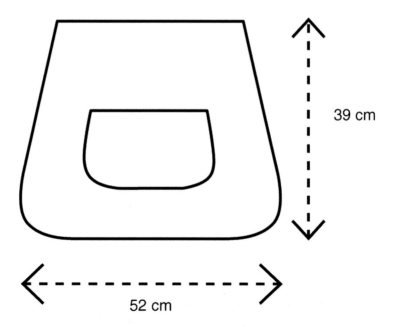

39 cm

52 cm

Handles

Select a colour or a mixture of colours and decide on the length and thickness of your handles.

1

1 Dunk the fleece of one handle into a bowl filled with warm soapy water, but keep both ends of the handle dry – this is important throughout the felting process, as the ends will be felted directly onto the bag.
(NB: To keep the ends dry you can protect them with plastic or aluminium foil.)

2

2 Hold firmly and rub along the handle with both hands for five minutes, adding soap until it begins to felt. The wool should be wet but not soaked.

3

3 Roll back and forth in the bubble wrap for five minutes. Make sure to keep the ends dry.

4

4 Roll the handle for ten minutes, in between your hands, adding a little bit of water and soap.

Once the handle feels hard and compact, rinse with hot water, again ensuring the ends stay dry. Roll again for a few more minutes until the felting is finished, then rinse in cold water until all the soap has been removed.

Bag

1 Use the same shape for the project, or design your own template. Add 30% to the final size desired, to allow for shrinkage. Cut out two templates in foam underlay, one for the bag and one for the pocket.

1

2 Choose a colour or a mixture of colours of wool for the bag. Lay your wool in the same direction across the template, overhanging by 3 cm (1¼ in.) on three sides so as to be able to fold your 'seams'. At the top opening edge, leave the template underneath 1 cm higher than the fleece.

2

3 Wet the wool evenly with hot soapy water.

3

4 Cover the wool with bubble wrap and flatten it with both hands. Then turn everything over, holding tightly.

4

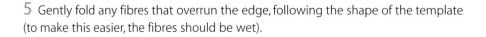

5 Gently fold any fibres that overrun the edge, following the shape of the template (to make this easier, the fibres should be wet).

6 Spread a layer of wool in the same direction as the other side. Wet and flatten it by pressing gently with your hands through the bubble wrap. Then turn it over, holding it tightly, and start to fold the edges as before. Repeat for your three layers criss-crossing each new one over the previous one. You can also use different colours for each layer, and if you want a very thick bag you can apply as many as six layers!

7 Place the template for the pocket where you want it, and cover it with two thin layers of wool, the top one at 90° to the first. Wet this lightly with soapy water except at the top (the opening of the pocket), which should remain free of fleece.

8 Design and add details to both sides of the bag using wool, fancy yarn and/or natural fibres.

9 When it is done, cover it with net. Wet it with warm soapy water and start to rub gently through the net. Do not exert too much pressure when rubbing, because it is still very fragile at this stage. Work on both sides for 15 minutes.

10 Rub the edges carefully, following the template. Work on the opening of the bag and pocket with the tips of your fingers and some soap by gently pressing in any loose fibres. Continue this for 15 minutes.

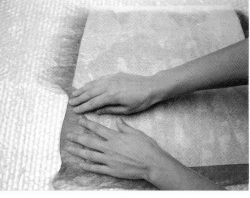

5

6

7

8

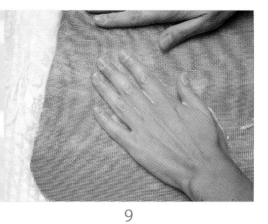

9

10

11 Place your handles where you want them, either inside or outside the bag. Spread the dry ends of each handle to ensure that they felt easily. Once again, cover the bag with the net and wet it.

11

12 Rub with soap for 15 minutes, concentrating on the handles.

12

13 Roll the bag up tightly in the bubble wrap and the straw mat. Exerting pressure with both hands, roll back and forth for five minutes. Unroll and gently stretch the fibres in order to flatten them out. Turn the bag through 90º and continue for 15 minutes.

13

14 Remove the template when the bag is starting to shrink. Flatten it by rubbing and pressing the 'seams' with one hand inside the bag and the other on the outside. Continue rolling for 15 minutes, changing direction every five minutes. Then check to see if the felting is complete by pinching the fibres – if you can still lift them, you should continue rolling – and comparing the size of the bag with the template.

14

15 Rinse in hot water, add soap and, this time using only the bubble wrap, keep on rolling for 15 minutes in both directions

15

16 The bag is now ready. Rinse in cold water. It's important to get rid of all the soap, as you may find white spots in the felt if the soap is not removed properly. Add a drop of vinegar to protect against moths. Then throw the felt against the table ten times to mat the fibres one more time. Stretch it into its final shape, flatten it, and let it dry overnight in a warm room.

16

how to make a hat

6

Hats are my passion – that is why I am a milliner! The most powerful and symbolic accessories in history, hats are a way of indicating a hierarchical position (for instance, the headgear of bishops or kings) or a social status (that of policemen or firemen).

Hats have also been adapted throughout history so as to be comfortable and to protect us against the environment and extreme weather. A hat will hold in 20% of body heat.

A good hat must find the right balance on the head, and be in the right proportions. It is essential in an outfit, as it changes the silhouette and causes light to fall on the face in a particular way.

This project entails making a stylish cloche hat with a small brim. The shape is inspired by the 1920s. Here I have used two layers of wool to obtain a certain fineness (50 g of wool in total), as befits a hat. Practical and timeless, I like this particular style because it is simple and suits a wide range of face shapes. I have also added a flower-pattern detail, which was pre-felted to ensure a sharp outline. It's a feature that can also be used on bags or cushions.

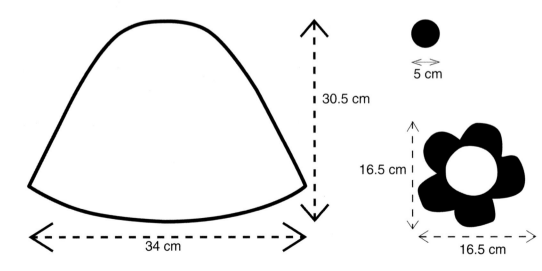

30.5 cm

5 cm

16.5 cm

34 cm

16.5 cm

When planning a hat it is very important to choose the right colours. Hold the coloured wools next to your face. Observe the quality of light they bring and choose those that suit you the best. Find out which of the colours harmonise best with the colours of your eyes, hair and skin.

1 Cut out the templates of the hat and the flower in foam underlay. Cut out the flower in thin felt of the desired colour. Put half the bubble wrap on the table and lay the hat template on it.

2 Spread the first layer evenly across the template, laying the fibres in the same direction. Remember to overlap the wool by about one third in the manner of roof tiles. Overrun the edge by at least 3 cm (1¼ in.), so as to be able to fold the 'seams'.

3 Add a second layer by laying the fibres at 90º to the first. Wet evenly with warm water and soap. Cover it with bubble wrap and flatten it gently with both hands. Remove any air bubbles, then turn over your work.

4 Lift the bubble wrap and carefully start to fold the overrunning fibres around the template. If the fibres are dry, don't hesitate to add hot soapy water. It helps!

5 Lay two layers as before, then wet and cover them with the bubble wrap. Turn the hat over, holding it tightly, and fold the edges around the template. It's important to take your time and to be very precise when folding the 'seams'.

6 Place the pre-felted flower where you want it, then place the net curtain over the top.

1

2

3

4

5

6

7 Wet with hot soapy water – the hat should be evenly damp though not yet soaking. If you put on too much water, mop it up with a sponge or a towel. Rub gently through the net for ten minutes with soapy hands. Your fleece needs to feel flat, and there should not be any air bubbles.

7

8 Roll up the felt hat tightly in the bubble wrap and the towel or straw mat. Exerting pressure with both hands, roll back and forth 25 times. Unroll and stretch in order to flatten out any pleats. Add hot soapy water if necessary. Check that the flower has remained in the right position, then turn the hat through 90° and roll it another 30 times. Repeat the rolling process for about 10 minutes, changing direction every three or four minutes.

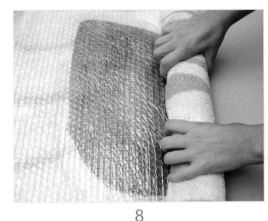

8

9 Rub and massage the felt directly for about 10-15 minutes with both hands, using a lot of soap. To obtain smooth edges, rub the wool following the shape of the template.

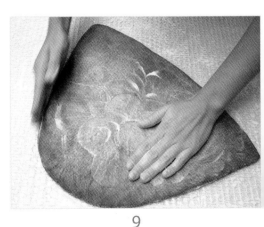

9

10 When the felt has started to shrink, the template becomes too large and should be taken out. Cut the base of the hat and remove it.

10

11 Rub and flatten your 'seams' with one hand inside and the other outside the hat. Apply pressure until it feels smooth and flat. Repeat step 8, adding hot soapy water. Roll the felt in the bubble wrap and towel until the felt is firm and difficult to pull. Finally, throw the felt about 10 times against the table. This allows a final contraction of fibres and offers some real personal satisfaction after such hard work! Rinse the felt with cold water, leaving no trace of soap. Add a drop of vinegar to protect against moths.

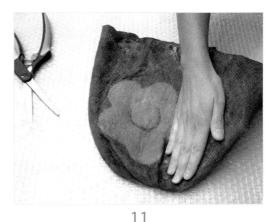

11

12 While your felt is still damp, start to mould the hat using a hot iron (wool setting) and a wet cotton cloth, to get a lot of steam so that you can shape it. Stretch the felt over a hat block or any reasonable alternative. You can find and use all sort of shapes as a hat block – for instance, a pan or a plastic bowl. Attach the felt to the mould with an elastic band or a piece of string. Leave it to dry overnight. Once dry, remove the hat from the mould and stitch or cut the brim! NB: Remember that felt doesn't fray. You can add details such as beads, sequins or embroidery.

12

7 how to make a scarf

The colours and the fineness of the wool are two essentials for anyone aiming to make a beautiful-quality scarf. When planning one for yourself, place the skeins of coloured wool next to your face, carefully observing the light each one reflects on your skin, hair and eyes.

In the end, you should choose the one you feel is most harmonious with your own colouring, but as a guide, pinks, fuchsias and purples are colours that are suitable for many people – they illuminate with a flattering light; greens must be the right tone – otherwise they can make you look ill; black is a bit difficult in my opinion, because it brings with it a lot of shadows and only suits some people; whites light up – but be careful if you have a very light skin complexion; oranges are warm; and blues are cold.

Every colour has its own peculiarities, and creates a very particular atmosphere. Colour is a journey of discovery which we must embark upon boldly and without prejudice.

As for fineness, to get a very fine felt, you need to spread the fibres thinly and evenly. At the same time, take care to avoid weaknesses. If there are to be any holes, they ought to be intentional! For this project I used 55 g (2 oz) of wool in total.

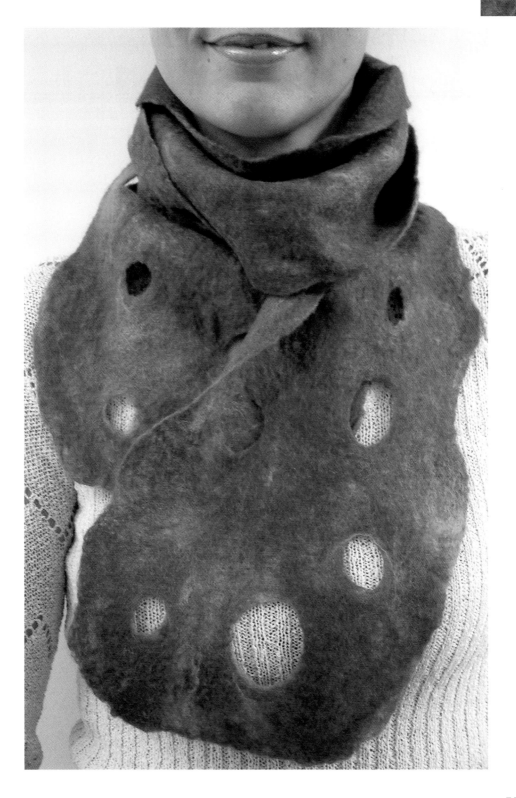

1 Use combs to mix different colours of wool to create unique shades. You can add all sorts of natural fibres such as bamboo, silk, soya, and synthetic fibres (though these will need to be lightly covered with wool before they will felt properly).

2 Spread a layer of fine wool in one direction. Overlap the fibres by a third to avoid any parts being too thin.

3 It is essential to have an even surface. Check with your hands that the fibres are properly laid, adding or removing wool where necessary.

4 The originality of this scarf is the making of intentional holes in the felt! Design the scarf by carefully parting the wool with the tips of your fingers. Make holes of various sizes, keeping in mind that it will shrink when felted.

5 Place the net over a part of the scarf (because of the length it's easier to work on one part at a time) and wet it with hot soapy water. It should be evenly damp but not soaking wet. With your hands and some soap start to rub gently over the net for 10 to 15 minutes. Continue down the entire length of the scarf.

6 Roll the scarf firmly in the bubble wrap and straw mat, attaching the roll as you did in the cushion workshop, to make it easier to roll back and forth. Roll it 100 times, then unroll, flatten and stretch the fibres. Add hot soapy water, where necessary. Then put it back in the mat, and roll 200 times. It is important to alternate rolling along the length and the width, so as to have a steady shrinkage. Fold your scarf and the bubble wrap in half so as to be able to roll the width. Continue rolling for 10 minutes.

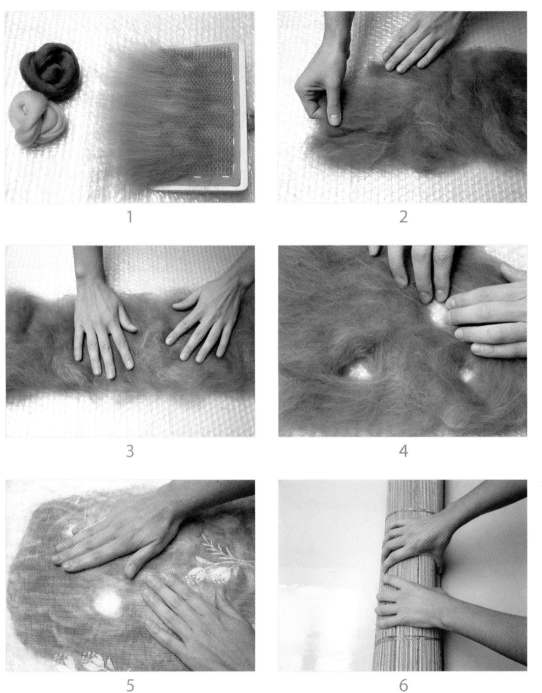

1

2

3

4

5

6

7 Unroll your scarf and if the fleece is dry, add hot water and soap. Remove the net and gently rub the holes with your fingertips for a few minutes. Check that no fibre is blocking the holes. Repeat the rolling process for a further ten minutes.

7

8 Massage around the shape of the scarf for five minutes, tucking in any loose fibres with soapy hands. Carry on rolling in the bubble wrap and mat for another ten minutes.

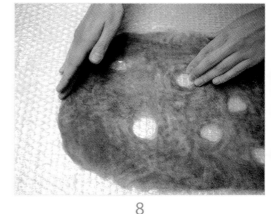

8

9 Rinse in hot water, then remove the excess water.

9

10 Roll up the scarf, this time in just the straw mat (folded in half lengthwise), then roll it back and forth for five minutes.

10

11 Now roll it widthways for five minutes. Continue until the felt feels firm and difficult to pull.

11

12 The felt is finished. Stretch it, flatten it and iron it on the wool setting until you have achieved a smooth surface. Then lay it flat and leave it to dry in a warm place.

12

 # 8 felt with children

Felt is a wonderful medium of expression that is specially suited for children to work with. Eco-friendly, soft and easy to use, wool can be compared to pencils and paint. The use of soap and water adds to the fun of this wet technique. I work with many children between the ages 3 and 17, and I always notice how much they appreciate felt as a way of expressing their creativity. My daughter is two and a half years old and loves felt-making. She never tires of getting her hands wet, scrubbing with soap and marvelling about these little bits of wool. In answer to the question, when is it suitable for a child to begin felt-making, I would say, once they have stopped putting everything in their mouth!

Any theme you can imagine will lend itself to producing pieces and articles in felt. You can, for example, connect the workshops with a child's school curriculum or tell a story.

This allows them to learn in a stimulating, creative and relaxing environment.

In this chapter you will find various ideas developed and a gallery of pictures of wonderful felt works made by the children.

Puppet

Create your 3D puppet with coloured wool, bearing in mind that the suggested template is a base that ought to be adjusted and improved. For instance, you might want to add ears or horns or wings. Working in 3D can be fun. To make the template, draw around the hand of the child, adding about 30% to allow for shrinkage.

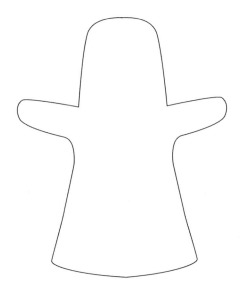

1 Spread two layers of fibres over the template, the second one at 90° to the first. Overlap the template by 2 cm (¾ in.).

2 Wet the wool extensively with hot soapy water and cover with bubble wrap. Then press gently with your hands to flatten the fibres.

3 Turn the work over and fold the overrunning fibres around the template.

4 Spread a further two layers of fibres, again at 90° to each other, but this time without overrunning the template.

5 Wet the wool, cover with bubble wrap and flatten.

6 Now draw the eyes, mouth and hair with wool of different colours. Add some hot water and soap, and cover with net.

7 With your hands, rub some soap through the net for 15 minutes, on both sides.

8 Wrap the puppet firmly in the bubble wrap and towel.

9 Roll it for five minutes, pressing down with your hands.

10 Unroll and check that everything is in place. Add hot water if necessary.

11 Repeat step 9 until the felt shrinks.

12 Remove the template by cutting the base.

13 Carry on rolling until the felt becomes difficult to stretch.

14 Rinse in cold water and then squeeze all the water out.

15 Shape the puppet into its final form by putting one hand inside it.

16 Let it dry, overnight in a warm place.

17 Add details using buttons and ribbons.

Teddy bear

From the template, make a unique customised teddy bear.

1 Following the workshop for the 'flat piece' (see page 29), felt two pieces measuring 25 x 30 cm (10 x 12 in.). On one of them add the nose and paws using different colours.

2 When the felt is dry, pin the template and cut the front and the back of the teddy bear.

3 Sew the two pieces together with a strong thread, leaving an opening to be filled with wool.

4 Fill up the teddy with wool and stitch up the opening.

5 Embroider the mouth and the eyes, then add details using beads and buttons.

Collective wall hanging

This workshop is all about using your imagination. It's a great way to tell a story or a legend, to make a magic carpet, a giant game to play together or a world map.

1 Decide on a theme – for example, portraits of the family, the solar system or a story from the school curriculum. Ask the children to draw each section of the theme in colour.

2 Prepare some pre-felted wool in different colours, cut all sorts of shapes and start to design trees, planets, characters… whatever you have chosen.

3 Each child should choose and felt a scene (see the flat-piece workshop on page 29) that tells a section of the story. They can felt individually or together in groups.

4 When the felt is thoroughly dry, add details using all kinds of materials. Embroider with coloured yarn and add sequins, beads, etc.

5 Finally, sew all the pieces together.

Beads

Necklaces and bracelets made of felted beads – original and very pleasant to make.

1 Using several colours, felt all kinds of balls in different sizes (see the ball workshop, page 80). You can add details with the felting needle.

2 Use a large needle and a thin elastic to assemble the beads and create necklaces and bracelets. Make a strong knot to finish.

Other children's designs

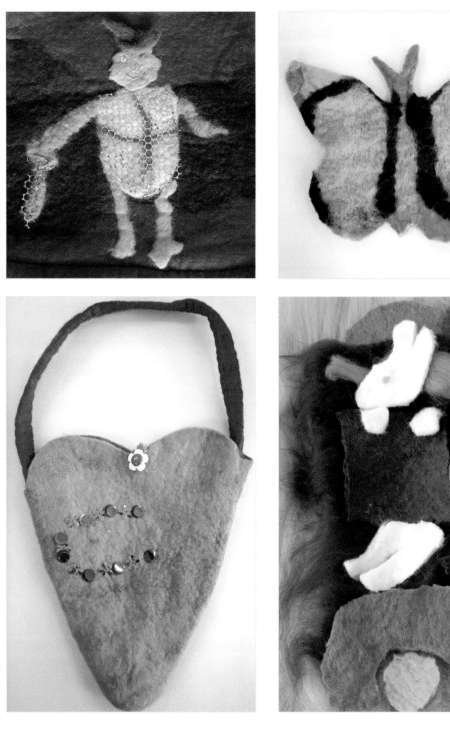

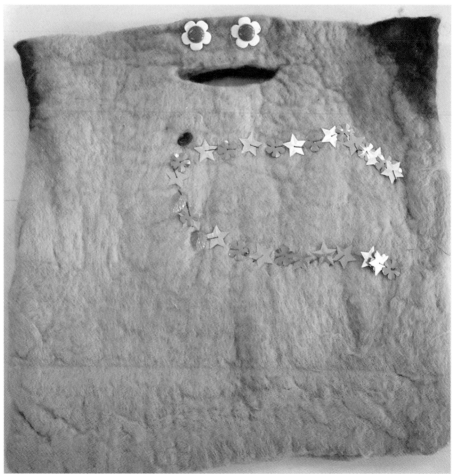

9 felt decorations

I have always loved parties and celebrations. I take great pleasure in making original gifts and decorations. In this chapter what you have already learned will help you to create unique gifts for your loved ones, as well as beautiful decorations to brighten up your parties. Make your own stars, snowflakes, snowman, Christmas trees and beautiful Christmas balls. Felt a pillow with a message of love for Valentine's Day. Make flower brooches, necklaces and bracelets to offer to your favorite friends. Felt offers the freedom to paint, sculpt and decorate to infinity. Here are some examples.

Stars and Christmas tree

1 Felt a large piece of wool in the colour(s) you desire.

2 When it is dry, cut two star or Christmas-tree shapes.

3 Prepare a gold or silver thread to attach the loop, and make a knot.

4 Embroider the two pieces together with the same colour thread, leaving a small opening to be filled with wool.

5 Once filled, sew on sequins and beads.

Snowflake

1 Felt a flat piece of white wool.

2 When it's dry, draw the shape of a snowflake on the felt with a pencil. You will then need a very sharp pair of scissors.

3 Carefully cut out the shape, then make a small hole and add a loop with some yarn.

Cushion with a message of love

1 Felt a flat piece of wool in the colour you have chosen for the letters. It is important to make the felt thin enough that the letters can be easily felted onto the background.

2 Cut out all the letters of your message, making sure that they are readable and understandable. Then spread two or three layers of wool for the background (depending on the thickness desired) and lay the letters and other decorations on top.

3 Cover with net and start to felt, paying particular attention to the letters and other decorations.

4 Once the letters have gripped the background, start rolling the felt.

5 Repeat the cushion workshop to make the cushion.

Flower brooch

Flowers are a topic of endless inspiration. To help you get started, keep some photos or fresh flowers in front of you. There are several techniques.

The first is to cut the flat shape of a flower in three different sizes. Stitch them together, then add some beads and sequins at the heart of the flower.

The second method is to cut the flower petals one by one and assemble them with an invisible stitch.

The third approach is to draw and cut the profile of the flower you want to make in thick plastic. Then repeat the relevant part of the hat workshop to obtain a 3D flower.

NB: It is possible to make the stem in advance and to felt it as a handle, as you did in the bag workshop.

Snowman
(using a felting needle)

Using the felting needle we can make a flat felt piece, as well as a 3D felt piece. This technique is a good exercise if you're thinking of making felt sculptures.

1

1 Choose some white wool and start to make a ball by rolling it in the palm of your hand. Remember that the volume will diminish when you poke the fibres with the needle. Place the wool on a sponge or some folded foam underlay. Choose the thicker needle and start to prick the ball slowly, then with a faster rhythm. Roll the ball while pricking. The fibres will mingle and the ball will become thicker and firmer. At the same time the volume will diminish. So add more wool as you go on pricking and rolling.

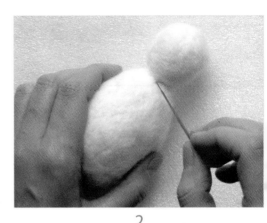

2

2 Sometimes the fleece sticks to the sponge or underlay. Pull it from time to time, and continue to prick. Make two balls, one large for the body and one small for the head.
Join them together using a thick needle.

3 With different coloured wool and a fine needle, draw the face and the nose.

4 Make a little scarf by pricking the wool with a fine needle.

5 Finish by adding the details of the scarf and the three buttons using a fine needle.

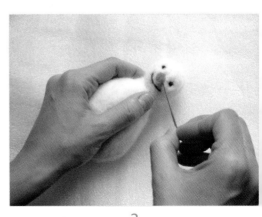

3

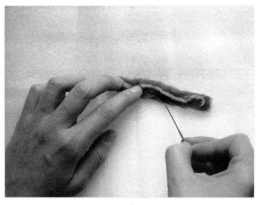

4

5

Balls

Felted balls are versatile and very easy to make. They are great for adding details to puppets, or for making buttons or beads for jewellery. They are also very therapeutic. People of all ages will enjoy this workshop.

1 Choose two or three different colours of wool. Select a piece to be your inside colour and dip it in warm soapy water.

1

2 Roll it between both hands without too much pressure. Keep dipping the wool regularly into the water, adding soap while rolling. It is important to have soaking-wet wool during the rolling process and to press gently. When the wool starts to felt, apply more pressure and keep rolling.

2

3 Wrap the ball in a different-colour wool and repeat the dipping and rolling process. Soap plays an important role, and it is essential to keep adding more throughout the process.

3

4 Once again, wrap the ball with a different colour wool.

4

5 Continue until you are satisfied with the size of the ball.

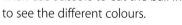

5

6 When it's done, rinse well in cold water to get rid of all the soap.
Then use scissors to cut the ball in two to see the different colours.

6

artists

Felt is an ancestral material that is also used in contemporary creations. In this chapter a number of artists have warmly agreed to share their individual visions of felt. Each one explains their relationship with felt and their passion for this wonderful expressive medium.

B. Bayanduuren (Mongolia)

Originally a painter and decorator, B. Bayanduuren started to work with felt in 1995. She is an artist and a teacher who has found her own methods and solutions using felt in a non-traditional way as a fine-art material. She likes to paint with fleece and has developed a range of felted works, paintings, wall-hangings, sculptures, dolls, clothes and accessories.

She has been exhibiting internationally and is the founder of the association of Mongolian felt-makers known as 'the white circle'.
Email:
bayan_duren@yahoo.com

Agostina Zwilling (Italy)

I am a felt-maker who wants to be a feel-maker. The medium and the techniques help me convey and to look deeper into my message, which is about human rights, violence and blood. Take courage, come up and see.
Email: agosta.zwilling@tiscali.it

Karoliina Arvilommi (Finland) *(below)*

I have been working with textiles and colours for over 20 years, first as a weaver, then for the last 15 years as a full-time independent felt-maker, concentrating on decorative art. Felt-making allows me the freedom of form and colour that I desire. It is such a liberating medium to work with, created by feel rather than calculation! Quality is an important aspect I have always strived for.
Email: rod@4felts.com

Annette Quentin-Stoll (Germany) (*left*)

Since learning felt-making in Finland in 1998, I have been fascinated by the possibility of creating 3D objects without any seams. One of my first pieces had a 'flexible pointed end', which was later used for hats, bags, toys and flower accessories. In my mind this shape is connected with the female body, and when I became pregnant in 2005, I made this wearable felt called Mama.
Email: filzdesign@gmx.de

May Jacobsen Hvistendahl (Norway) (*right*)

Felt is nature. Colour is for me the main inspiration in my work. This is why I hand-dye all my materials. Our lives are very urban, but felt connects us to the natural world. With my work I wish to make a difference in the lives of the people who wear it and who see it.
Email: mayhvistendahl@hotmail.com

Lori Flood (USA) (*left*)

With felt-making I can create seamless and multi-dimensional pieces which are free of the constraints dictated by weave or knit stitches. Surface designs can be added much like paint is brushed onto a canvas, and the ability to both sculpt and paint allows limitless opportunities to create beautiful textiles.
Email: spinterstreadle@hotmail.com

Mehmet Girgic (Turkey)

I began working as a felt craftsman in 1966 in my grandfather's shop. We mainly made traditional kepeneks (shepherds' cloaks) and felt rugs. Having learnt the craftsman's skills from my grandfather, I developed my own techniques for creating the tall conical felted hats worn by the Whirling Dervishes.

For many years, I've been teaching felt craftsmanship around the world and developing contemporary felt techniques. Painterly and mosaic techniques using felt are my most recent developments. These methods allow traditional Ottoman designs (the name derives from detailed Turkish embroidery created during the Ottoman period) as well as modern abstract work. Email: thefeltmaker@yahoo.com

Andrea Graham (Canada)

The art of felt-making connects me to the natural world and ancient culture. During the very physical felting and filling process, I often think of the ancient nomads, particularly the women and the sacred rituals of felt-making, which was central to their culture. I love than I can both sculpt and paint with wool. My options are limitless. My inspiration is the medium itself and the colours before me, the natural world, my own spiritual journey and the empowerment of women. Email: graham_andrea@cogeco.ca

Andrea Hunter (UK)

Andrea's felt pictures have depth, subtlety, texture and a real feeling of movement. This sense of movement is particularly evident in her windswept landscapes and images of animals. These qualities are born from her technique of working with fine layers of wool as if they were paint. She is inspired by the landscape and inhabitants of the Yorkshire Dales and particularly in the dramatic contrasts that the weather brings. UK: andrea@focusonfelt.co.uk

Liisa Kallam and Lisa Tomasberg (Estonia)

We have designed these cushions inspired by the untouched and wild Estonian landscape.

We used Estonian and Gotland wool, and they are stuffed with natural sea grass from the coast. We've been working together since 2001, focusing on interior textiles. The Estonian felting tradition is not very old, and we are both very excited to be researching this 'new' material! Email: liisakala@hot.ee

Sabine Fouchier (France)

Felt is the essence of all textiles. When making felt I connect to a universal and sacred dimension. I love to explore its qualities and to create unique fashion accessories. The felt pieces I make are intended to protect and express the traditions of our spiritual world. Wool has been felted ever since the discovery of fire. Today felt-making is as active as ever and continues to tell us the history of humankind.

Email: sabinechapeaux@yahoo.com

Wendy Fletcher (Australia)
(*left*)

Felting provides me with a surface that is soft, strong and durable – qualities needed for my figures. I use colour to unify the techniques and mediums. I find that the delicate merino fibres introduce minor colour subtlety. I trap and sew wool threads onto the surface during the felting process, to create a surface that is textured and yet easily machined and beaded. Email: cfletch@bigpond.net.au

Anna Gunnasdóttir (Iceland)

I am fond of using Icelandic wool for hand-felting. I find it excellent for making sculptures out of wool according to my imagination. My work depicts free Icelandic nature with its wild beauty. The shell forms I use most of the time come from the seashore, which is part of everyday life in Iceland. Email:anna.design@nett.is

appendix:
The Felt Art of the Mongols

My whole view of felt changed after I read *The Felt Art of the Mongols* by Dr Luntengiin Batchuluun. Dr Batchuluun led me to a better understanding of the lives of the 'felt-wall people', namely the nomadic people of Mongolia, which revealed to me both the origins and the sacred dimension of felt. In time I visited the country and spoke to him in depth about the place of felt in Mongolian society.

Through Dr Batchuluun's book we discover more than 265 words in the Mongolian language that relate to felt-making. However, to study the history of felt, as he has for more than three decades, is to study not just the history of one people but that of humankind. Such a study is based on several sources: oral tradition, research on historical manuscripts, archaeological evidence, traditional objects still in use today, and cultural heritage.

The earliest forms of nomadic life in Central Asia date from 10,000 BC. In time human beings were able to domesticate five species of mammal: sheep, goats, horses, camels and cows. The Mongols are nomads who love their animals as if they were people. When they first began to domesticate sheep, they built an early form yurt around them to protect them from predators. A yurt is a large round felt-covered tent that has been the traditional dwelling for nomads in this region for at least 3500 years, and today is still used by around half of the population of Mongolia. We know from rock drawings found right across Central Asia that the process of domestication started with a sheep attached to a picket, which encouraged the rest of the flock to gather inside the enclosure, and such an apparently simple development in their cultural life is still an important part of the Mongolian national consciousness. The later discovery of fire enabled the nomads to heat the water to turn wool into felt. It is worth noting that, etymologically, the word for 'fire' in the Mongolian language is connected to the word for the main wooden stick used in the construction of the yurt.

Knowing how to build a felted yurt enabled the Mongols to be nomads, and the yurt is still the most powerful symbol of Mongolian culture. Felt is the ideal solution for the nomadic way of life. Its first advantage lies in being easy to produce; you need only fire, water and wool to make it. The second is that it's light, durable and easy to carry, and offers nomads the freedom to move when they feel like it. A felt tent, enclosing a fireplace, can be put up in the same time it takes them to make a pot of Mongolian tea. Lengths of bamboo or straw are used as needles to stitch the yurt together. The felt is then protected against wool-eating insects with the cream of fermented milk or a dry cheese.

Felt-making is still an important activity in Mongolian society, and the person who leads the felt-making in a community is invariably the chief of a tribe or head of a large family, someone who knows the shamanistic traditions. As Dr Batchuluun puts it, 'Only a man can direct the making of felt, since women in the shamanistic tradition must protect fertility. The fire has a strong power which, it is believed, can harm fertility.' In the same vein, there is also a tradition in Central Asia as a whole, linked to similar shamanistic beliefs, of making spiritual and totemic idols in felt for protection.

'When the felt is made, a celebration takes place,' says Dr Batchuluun. 'Poems are recited and taboos respected. People celebrate together the making of the new felt. Each participant must place the community interest before his own. The horse or camel is made ready and the felt is blessed with milk. The new felt is being born surrounded by the mother felt. But throughout the year, individuals are free to develop their own creative ideas for felt.'

Dr Batchuluun believes that felt is an invention of high technology, and the ideal solution for living in a climate where winter temperatures plummet to -30ºC. 'If we compare a five-metre wall made of iron with one made of felt,' he says, 'we find that iron, which is hard and impenetrable, does not protect against the cold as well as felt, which is soft and porous. But for Mongolians wool has a symbolic association with life itself. This material is magical as well as practical, and the yurt is an art work whose design is linked to the people's spiritual beliefs, which inform all aspects of life. It is also worth noting that Mongolians wear hats of a shape similar to the shape of a yurt – the yurt is around us just as the hat is around our head.'

As far as the symbolism and origin of certain colours is concerned, Dr Batchuluun informed me that, 'Mongolians choose blue and red. The sky is blue, and the water that surrounds life is a cold colour, and in between is the red of the fire. With a natural dye extracted from an insect of the grasshopper family we can also obtain green, while a tea plant is used to obtain a yellowish-brown.'

Dr Batchuluun also makes connections between different nomadic peoples of the northern hemisphere – such as Eskimos, the American Indians and the Mongols – that can be seen in structures like the yurt as well as other cultural traditions. 'We talk about the great movements of peoples. The shamanism of these people, their traditions and their art are closely linked. In Mongolia, there are tepees like those in North America. They are still used by the Tatsans, a small Mongolian tribe living with the reindeer that they ride and whose hides they use to make tepees. By studying the great Mongol ancestors, everything that has been forgotten in Mongolia can be rediscovered among the peoples of North America. Notice how the shape of an igloo looks strangely like a yurt. In the same way, if we want to write the story of felt, it is not the story of one nation but a universal story.'

glossary

Biodegradable Capable of being broken down naturally into environmentally harmless products once in contact with a biologically active environment.

Blocking The process of moulding a hat shape.

Cloche A brimless, close-fitting woman's hat from the 1920s.

Carding The process of disentangling and spreading the fibres of a fleece, using rollers or a flat surface covered with wires or iron teeth, thereby removing impurities such as mud or straw.

Combing The process of separating and straightening fibres using combs, so that they run in the same direction.

Comb A machine or hand tool which removes short fibres and vegetable matter, and aligns the fibres.

Dyeing Modification of the original colour of a material by the use of a dissolved or dispersed substance, either natural or synthetic.

Felt A matted fabric made by rolling and pressing wool, hair or fur in hot water. The fibres intermingle and interlock, creating a durable material that doesn't fray when cut.

Felting needle A needle with rough, notched edges that poke the fibres so as to entangle them with other fibres and create felt. Originally used for industrial felt.

Flax A plant that produces linen.

Fleece The shorn wool or coat of an animal.

Fibre Natural fibres are of animal (wool, cashmere, etc.), mineral (asbestos) or vegetable origin (linen, cotton); they can also be man-made: rayon, nylon and polyester are produced by the polymerisation of synthetic chemicals.

Fine Fibre assessed to be the thinnest in diameter within a breed or flock.

Hat block A wooden form used as a mould to shape a hat by hand.

Keratin A chemical substance of which animal fibre is composed.

Lanolin A product recovered from the refining of wool grease, used in cosmetics and ointments.

Loom A machine for producing cloth by the interlacing of threads at right angles.

Merino The finest and highest-quality wool.

Micron (or micrometre) A unit of length, a thousandth part of one millimetre, or one millionth of a metre. The thickness of a fibre is measured in microns.

Milliner An artisan who makes and sells hats.

Millinery The craft of making hats.

Mother felt In Mongolia, an old felt used in place of a mat on which a new felt is made (called the 'daughter felt').

pH factor The measure of acidity or alkalinity of a particular substance.

Shrinking factor The proportion by which a piece of cloth or other material becomes smaller when wetted.

Silk The end product of silk moths. The cocoon of a silk moth, cultivated or wild, is the only natural fibre that comes in filament form.

Soybean fibre A protein-based fibre produced from the soybean.

Tops Commercially prepared fibres produced by carding and combing the fibres into parallel strips of similar length, they are ideal for felt-making

Yarn A collection of fibres or filaments twisted together to form a continuous strand. Natural or man-made, yarn has many applications, including knitting and weaving.

Yurt (or ger) A round felt tent with a wooden structure, used by nomadic people in Central Asia.

Woolmark The registered IWS (International Wool Secretariat) trademark denoting products made from pure new wool.

suppliers of fibres, dyes and equipment

UK

www.winghamwoolwork.co.uk
tel: + 44 (0) 1226 742926
fax: +44 (0) 1226 741166
Freepost
70 Main Street,
Wentworth, Rotherham,
South Yorkshire S62 7BR

www.handweaversstudio.co.uk
tel: + 44 (0) 208 521 2281
29 Haroldstone Road,
London E17 7AN

www.moralfibre.uk.com
tel: + 44 (0) 1584 856654
Church Farm Studios,
Stanton Lacy,
Ludlow SY8 2AE

www.craftynotions.com
tel: + 44 (0) 1636 700862
Unit 2, Jessop Way,
Newark NG24 2ER

www.shetland-wool-brokers-zetnet.co.uk
tel: + 44 (0) 1595 693579
Dept E, 90 North Road, Lerwick,
Shetland ZE1 0PQ

www.fibrecrafts.com
tel: + 44 (0) 1483 565800
fax: + 44 (0) 1483 565807
Old Portsmouth Road,
Peasmarsh, Guildford,
Surrey GU3 1LZ

www.scottishfibres.co.uk
tel: + 44 (0) 131 445 3899
23 Damhead, Lothianburn,
Edinburgh EH10 7EA

www.omegadyes.co.uk
tel: + 44 (0) 1453 823691
3–5 Regent Street,
Stonehouse, Gloucestershire GL10 2AA

www.textiledyes.co.uk
www.kemtex.co.uk
tel: + 44 (0) 1257 230225
fax: + 44 (0) 1257 230225
Kemtex Colours,
Chorley Business and Technology Centre,
Euxton Lane, Chorley,
Lancashire PR7 6TE

www.handspin.co.uk
tel: + 44 (0) 1303 862617
Hilltop, Windmill Cross,
Canterbury Road, Lyminge,
Folkestone, Kent CT18 8HD

www.hatblocks.co.uk
tel: +44 (0) 1902 893683
Guy Morse-Brown (hat blocks)
Mill Lane Farmhouse,
Wombourne,
Staffordshire WV5 0LE

Australia

www.treetopscolours.com.au
tel: + 61 (8) 9387 3007
fax: +61 (8) 9387 1747
Tree Tops Colour Harmonies
6 Benwee Road, Floreat
Western Australia 6014

Finland

www.piiku.fi
tel: + 35 814 856319
Piesalantilantie 17,
41900 Petajavesi,
Finland

USA

Fibres / Needles

www.bluegooseglen.com

www.desertweyr.com

www.rhlindsaywool.com

www.sweetgrasswool.com

www.ashandbay.com

www.louet.com

Yarns

www.cascadeyarns.com

www.bluemoonfiberarts.com

Combs and cards

www.foxglovefiber.com

www.howardbrush.com

www.strauchfiber.com

Canada

Fibres / Needles

www.louet.com

Yarns

www.pickupsticksonline.com

France

Fibres / Needles

www.paindepices.fr

www.atelier-de-kitty.com

www.creava.com

www.mouton-feutre.com

references

Bibliographical references

Batchuluun, L., *The Felt Art of the Mongols* (Ulan Bator, Mongolian University of Arts and Culture, 2003)

Burkett, M.E., *The Art of the Felt Maker* (Abbot Hall Gallery, Cumbria, 1979)

Fritz, A., *The Fibre of Clothing*, (Oxford University Press, 1980)

Marcon, E., & Mongini, M., *World Encyclopedia of Animals* (Black Cat, 1984)

Walsh, P., *The Yarn Book* (London: A & C Black, 2006)

Mongolie, les fils de Gengis Khan, GEO magazine no. 135/mai 1990 un nouveau monde: la Terre

Echoes (IFA magazine) : issue 80 K.Arvilommi // Finland (p15) Mirka Dolls // Australia (22)

Echoes: issue 87 A.Zwilling // Italy (p10) Taking a leap // Canada (p12)

Echoes: issue 86 A.Quentin-Stoll at play // Germany (p17) A.Hunter's work (p2 + back cover)

Echoes: issue 78 World Festival of Felt // Hungary (p18/19)

Echoes: issue 85 Shirmel embroidery Mongolia (p8)

Echoes: issue 84 A.Gunnarsdóttir // Iceland (p18/19)

Links

www.woolfest.co.uk (wool & fibres festival, England)

www.feltmakers.com (The International Feltmakers Association)

www.hermitagemuseum.org

www.moutonvillage.info (french tourist park themed around sheep)

www.bergerie-nationale.educagri.fr (wool & felt festival, France)

www.latoisondart.net (wool & felt festival, France)

www.selvedge.org (textile magazine)

http://estivales.duchapeau.free.fr/index.htm (hat festival, France)

Other sources of information

Musée du Feutre
Mairie, Place du Colombier
08120 Mouzon
France
Tel: 00 33 (0)324261063
Email:
musee.atelier.du.feutre@wanadoo.fr

White Circle: Felt Art Centre
Mongolian Feltmakers Association
PO Box 155
Ulanbator 211022
Mongolia
Emails: whitecircle_mn@yahoo.com
        bayan_duuren@yahoo.com

index